# Iron Willpower: How to Build Grit, Develop Self-Discipline, and Master Self-Control

## By Dominic Mann

# Table of Contents

Iron Willpower: How to Build Grit, Develop Self-Discipline, and Master Self-Control

# Introduction

*"The one quality which sets one man apart from another — the key which lifts one to every aspiration while others are caught up in the mire of mediocrity — is not talent, formal education, nor intellectual brightness — it is self-discipline.*

*"With self-discipline all things are possible.*

*"Without it, even the simplest goal can seem like the impossible dream."*
*— Theodore Roosevelt, 26th President of the United States*

In 2007, a study was conducted by Richard Wiseman from the University of Bristol. The study involved 3,000 people and their New Year's resolutions. At the beginning, the majority of the study's participants were confident of success.

Nonetheless, 88 percent failed. Although the majority were initially confident of success, only 12 percent succeeded. One in ten!

Other studies and surveys have repeatedly shown that people feel that the number one reason for failing to follow through on a goal or new habit is a lack of willpower.

Not only does a lack of willpower leave New Year's resolutions unfulfilled, but also ambitious dreams of massive success. People find themselves ruled not by their desire for success and greatness, but ruled by petty bodily desires, wants, appetites, and emotions. Almost all of us feel that our lack of self-discipline is preventing us from achieving our full potential — and, as I know from personal experience, that is an immensely frustrating feeling.

We often find ourselves succumbing to the allure of instant gratification rather than sticking it out and tediously working toward greatness.

However, if we do wish to achieve greatness in life, we must find a way to overcome this dilemma. As Jim Rohn once said:

*"Discipline is the bridge between goals and accomplishment."*

Many of us have goals, dreams, ambitions, and hopes. However, we must commit ourselves to our goals in life, and then toil away at them. As Haile Gebrselassie said:

*"Once you have commitment, you need the discipline and hard work to get you there."*

The key to success in life is having the self-discipline and willpower to stick it out. The majority of people find themselves living mediocre lives because they either settle for what's "good enough" or give up at the first sign of difficulty. To succeed, we must find a way to overcome short-sighted temptations and learn to prevail in the face of difficulty.

You might have heard of the following famous expression:

*"When the going gets tough, the tough gets going."*

In other words, when things get difficult, the strong will work even harder to meet the challenge. Or, as Martin Luther King, Jr. put it more eloquently:

*"The ultimate measure of a man is not where he stands in moments of comfort and convenience, but where he stands at times of challenge and controversy."*

This problem — struggling with self-discipline and willpower — that so many of us encounter each and every day is exactly what you will learn to overcome and resolve as you read this book.

As we develop self-discipline, we become independent of external events, interferences, and temptations. We no longer need to postpone working toward our goals until the time is "just right." We build a fortress within, a fortress of self-discipline that is immune to difficulties, obstacles, temptations, and bodily desires. As Stephen R. Covey said:

*"Only the disciplined are truly free. The undisciplined are slaves to moods, appetites and passions."*

When we lack self-discipline, we become the equivalent of a dog tied to a cart. We go wherever the cart goes — the cart representing our moods, appetites, and desire for instant gratification

In this book, we will explore the best hacks and techniques to develop self-discipline and willpower. Continuing the previous analogy of the dog and the cart, you will learn to become a dog that can go wherever it wants. A dog that is independent of the cart. A dog that, if need be, pulls the cart around, rather than having the cart pull it around.

Although counterintuitive, discipline is freedom. When we lack self-control, we are ruled by our short-sighted primitive desires.

When we learn to master ourselves, we can do what we truly want. We rule ourselves. We decide what we want to do, and do it. We act according to what we think, as opposed to acting according to how we feel at that particular point in time.

We become our own masters. We become the masters of our own fate. Or as William Ernest Henley would say:

*"I am the master of my fate. I am the captain of my soul."*

Likewise, Pietro Aretino, an Italian author, playwright, and poet during the 16th century, said the following:

*"I am, indeed, a king, because I know how to rule myself."*

Power comes from within.

So let's dive right in and learn to conquer ourselves, so that we can, in turn, conquer the world.

# Chapter 1: Willpower as a Muscle

Building self-discipline is the same as learning to play the piano, swim, or drive a car. It's the same as building any other skill. Self-discipline is a learned behavior.

Regularly exercise self-control throughout life, and it will become easier and easier.

Willpower is like a muscle. Regularly exercise it, and it grows stronger. Never use it, and it will atrophy.

While this might seem disheartening at first, we can use this fact to our advantage. Our willpower is not set. Those of us who feel that we have no willpower and lack control over ourselves can take heart in the fact that we can build it up. We can grow our willpower, making it stronger.

We can also practice self-discipline in certain areas of our life, and as it grows stronger and stronger, we can apply the same self-discipline to all areas of life. We develop our overall self-discipline. Just as we can use strong biceps for other things other than lifting weights at the gym.

### Running Out of Willpower

In 1998, Roy F. Baumeister and three other researchers from Case Western Reserve University baked some fresh chocolate chip cookies, making sure to fill the building with their delicious aroma. Once they had baked the yummy cookies and put them on a tray, they got a bowl and filled it with comparatively unappetising radishes. They then put the bowl of radishes next to the tray of freshly baked chocolate chip cookies.

The researchers then got three groups of people participating in the study. The first group would eat the cookies. The second group would have to force themselves to eat "at least two or three radishes." The third group — the control group — would do nothing, unaware of this whole radish versus cookie thing.

Understandably, the second group was a little upset. As the study reports, many of the radish-eaters "exhibit[ed] clear interest in the chocolates, to the point of looking longingly at the chocolate display and in a few cases even picking up the cookies to sniff at them."

After this epic feat of willpower, the radish-eaters — along with the other two groups — did a puzzle. The puzzle, unknown to the participants, was unsolvable.

The researchers then timed how long it took for the people from the three different groups to quit the puzzle.

The results?

The radish-eaters gave up solving the puzzle in less than half the time of the other two groups. Furthermore, they made far fewer attempts and, after the puzzle, reported being more tired than the chocolate-eaters and non-eaters.

The conclusion is that by using their willpower to not eat the delicious cookies, the radish-eaters had less willpower left to exert on the impossible puzzle. The willpower depletion resulting from denying themselves of cookies made them give up more easily on the subsequent puzzle task. Those that ate the cookies, or were ignorant of the whole cookie versus radish dilemma (i.e. the non-eaters), didn't have their willpower taxed. Consequently, they showed no decreased persistence in the puzzle.

Likewise, a separate study that had participants suppress emotions and not laugh at a humorous video clip saw them solve far fewer problems afterwards than those who had been allowed to laugh freely.

So what does all of this mean for us?

Well, as we will explore in Chapter 6, this means that we should be very intentional about what we choose to exert willpower on.

For example, if you want to exercise, do it first thing in the morning before anything has the chance to deplete your willpower. Likewise, if you are on a diet, throw out all your unhealthy food so it doesn't have the opportunity to tempt you.

## Building and Strengthening Willpower

One of the biggest ramifications of these willpower depletion studies is that willpower is like a muscle. If, for example, you take freezing cold showers each morning, eat dozens of radishes for breakfast, and run ten miles all before going to work, you will build up and strengthen your willpower. The first few days and weeks might be tough, but after several months, you will adjust. Your willpower will strengthen. Most importantly, you will be able to apply this same willpower to other areas of your life.

In fact, studies prove the fact that — just like a muscle — when exhausted in the short-term, willpower builds up its strength in the long-term.

A 1999 study asked participants to monitor and improve their posture for two weeks. If they caught themselves slouching or not standing up straight, they were to correct their posture. After the two weeks, those that worked on their posture "showed significant improvement" in willpower.

Likewise, people who engaged in minor acts of willpower, such as using their opposite hand and refraining from swearing, saw an increase in willpower after two weeks. As a 2006 paper reported:

*"To increase self-regulatory strength, participants were asked to perform some tasks for 2 weeks that involved self-regulation but had no direct relationship to [other forms of willpower]. One assignment was to use the participant's nonpreferred hand for a list of activities that included brushing teeth, stirring drinks, using a computer mouse, carrying items, eating, and opening doors. Another assignment involved verbal self-regulation in a series of prescribed ways: avoid curse words, speak in complete*

sentences, say only "yes" and "no" instead of using colloquial substitutes such as "yeah" and "nope," and refrain from starting sentences with "I." A control group performed no exercises. The laboratory sessions were conducted before and after the 2-week program. Once again, **the self-control exercises made people subsequently less vulnerable to [willpower] depletion**, as indicated by improvement in their performance on solving anagrams."

As if those studies were not enough, another two studies have shown different applications of the same fact: Willpower is like a muscle and is strengthened with use.

A 2010 study showed, in the words of the researchers, that "self-control performance may be improved by the regular practice of small acts of self-control." In this particular study, the researchers showed that "participants who practiced self-control by **cutting back on sweets** or **squeezing a handgrip** exhibited significant improvement" in willpower after two weeks of the self-control exercises. Conversely, the study's participants that "practiced tasks that did not require self-control" saw no improvement.

Similarly, in a 2007 study researchers gave participants "transparent boxes of chocolate Hershey's Kisses and instructed participants to keep the chocolates with them, but not to eat them, for 48 h." Take a bunch of delicious chocolates around with you for 48 hours? In a transparent box so you can see them in all their tasty glory? What a feat of willpower that must have been.

What the researchers found was that those who resisted the chocolates were much more capable of resisting other temptations in life, too. So, carry around something tempting, manage to resist the craving, and by constantly saying "no", you boost your ability to resist all other temptations.

By repeatedly exercising your willpower, you train yourself to become more self-disciplined in general. You only need to do the smallest things to build up your willpower.

Take the stairs rather than the elevator. Rather than just chucking your dirty dishes in the sink, wash them straight away. Brush your teeth with your opposite hand. Carry a little bag of yummy, tempting chocolates around with you.

Do little things like this regularly and you will strengthen your self-discipline.

# Chapter 2: Be on a Mission

Those among us that have the biggest successes and seem to wield the greatest willpowers all have a mission. They have a burning desire, something that transcends the self. It's not that these people were born with massive self-discipline. It's not that their genetics give them immense willpower. It's none of that.

They have a burning desire raging within them. They are on a mission.

As Friedrich Nietzsche, a 19th century philosopher, said:

*"He who has a **'why'** to live can bear almost any **'how'**."*

Have a mission. A purpose. A meaning. Have a "WHY". When you do, and you have an immense burning desire, you will overcome anything and everything. You will die trying. You will rise above all difficulties and surmount all obstacles, no matter what. You can bear any "HOW".

People will look to you and find themselves astonished at your seemingly superhuman willpower and self-discipline. The reality, however, is that you are simply pursuing that which you have a burning desire for. You are on a mission.

When you are working toward a worthwhile goal, something that you truly have a burning desire for, you will never quit. You will work through any amount of pain and effort. You need to have a mission.

## Navy SEALs

The defining event during the training to become a Navy SEAL is Hell Week. It is held early on, in the 3rd week of the First Phase. As Hell Week usually sees 90 percent of sailors quit, this prevents the Navy making an expensive investment in SEAL operational training for sailors who are not mentally and physically strong enough to become a SEAL.

So what's Hell Week?

Hell Week has you do five and a half days of operational training. It's cold, wet, brutal, and difficult. During the entire week, you get less than four hours of sleep.

Hell Week tests pain and cold tolerance, attitude, mental toughness, physical endurance, teamwork, and your ability to perform under immense physical and mental stress as well as sleep deprivation. And above all else, Hell Week tests your desire and determination.

Coming out of Hell Week — if they make it through without quitting — they realize that they are capable of 20 times more than they had ever thought possible.

Much research has been done over the years in an attempt to determine what the common trait among those who make it through Hell Week is.

The result?

It's not necessarily the fastest swimmers. Not the strongest men. Not the largest, biggest men. Rather, the common trait among those that stick it out through Hell Week is a burning desire to become a SEAL. The instructors note that they have observed only a single true predictor of which candidates will end up making it through: Those that want it the most. Instructors claim they can see how bad they want it, their burning desire in their eyes!

Being a big muscled guy isn't necessarily of much use when repeatedly subjected to mentally and physically crushing workouts. Being a good swimmer isn't necessarily enough to get you through the dozens of miles they must swim through freezing, rough surf. Being a capable athlete isn't necessarily enough to get you through having to run along the beach and roll in sand and mud. All in full gear.

They have sand burning in their eyes. Sand making their skin raw. Mud all over their faces and uniforms. Whenever they move, sand chafes their legs, raking over their open sores and wounds. They eat 7,000 calories each day yet still lose weight.

Nonetheless, it's not physical endurance that leads to success. As a BUD/S (Basic Underwater Demolition/SEAL) instructor at the San Diego facility said:

*"The belief that BUD/S is about physical strength is a common misconception. Actually, it's 90 percent mental and 10 percent physical. [Students] just decide that they are too cold, too sandy, too sore or too wet to go on.* **It's their minds that give up on them***, not their bodies."*

These guys have decided that they will do whatever it takes — no matter how hard, no matter how difficult — to achieve their goal. No sacrifice is too great.

In fact, they want their goal so bad — they have such an immense desire to succeed —

that they are literally willing to kill themselves. **They are willing to die trying**.

In an interview, the Navy SEAL who killed Osama bin Laden described the following scene during Hell Week:

*"One of the tests is they make you dive to the bottom of a pool and tie five knots,"* the Shooter *[of Osama bin Laden] says. "One guy got to the fifth knot and blacked out underwater. We pulled him up and he was, like, dead. They made the class face the fence while they tried to resuscitate him. The first words as he spit out water were 'Did I pass? Did I tie the fifth knot?' The instructor told him, 'We didn't want to find out if you could tie the knots, you asshole, we wanted to know how hard you'd push yourself. You killed yourself. You passed.'"*

Eric Greitens, a Navy SEAL, wrote a piece for the Wall Street Journal titled _An Inside Look at the SEAL Sensibility_. He wrote the following about the training that reduced his class of 220 wannabe SEALs to 21 graduates:

"When they really wanted to torture us, they'd say, 'Anybody who quits right now gets hot coffee and doughnuts. Come on, who wants a doughnut? Who wants a little coffee?'

[...]

"What kind of a man makes it through Hell Week? That's hard to say. But I do know—generally—who won't make it. There are a dozen types that fail: the weight-lifting meatheads who think that the size of their biceps is an indication of their strength, the kids covered in tattoos announcing to the world how tough they are, the preening leaders who don't want to get their hands dirty, and the look-at-me former athletes who have always been told they are stars but have never been pushed beyond the envelope of their talent to the core of their character.

[...]

"Some men who seemed impossibly weak at the beginning of SEAL training—men who puked on runs and had trouble with pull-ups—made it. Some men who were skinny *and short and whose teeth chattered just looking at the ocean also made it. Some men who were visibly afraid, sometimes to the point of shaking, made it too."*

Greitens explains those who survived the training all had one common trait:

*"Even in great pain, faced with the test of their lives, they had the ability to step outside of their own pain, put aside their own fear and ask: How can I help the guy next to me?"*

As Greitens described, those that succeeded were those that "dedicate[d] themselves to a higher purpose."

It's not just Navy SEALs who need — in Greitens words — "a higher purpose."

All of us, no matter what our goals, need that very same burning desire. That same "I'm on a mission" mentality. A higher purpose. When you have a mission, a higher purpose, you can muster willpower and self-discipline where previously there seemed to be none.

When you lack a clear mission, when you lack a higher purpose or life goal, you are much more easily seduced by the allure of temptations and the promise of instant-gratification.

<u>As Bad As You Want to Breathe</u>

A book titled *The Element: How Finding Your Passion Changes Everything* by world renowned creativity expert, Ken Robinson, recounts a story about commitment. Having listened to his brother performing in a band one night, Robinson decided to compliment the extraordinarily talented keyboard player:

*"Then I said that I'd love to be able to play keyboards that well. 'No, you wouldn't,' he responded. Taken aback, I insisted that I really would. 'No,' he said. 'You mean you like the idea of playing keyboards. If you'd love to play them, you'd be doing it.'"*

Many of us go through life with mild desires. I'd love to lose a bit of weight. I'd love to play the piano. I'd love to speak Chinese. I'd love to be a great tennis player. I'd love to be a great computer programmer.

But we never do any of those things. We don't truly have a burning desire for such things. Sure, they'd be nice, but we are not willing to put in the tremendous time and effort required to achieve those dreams. They are not goals, they are wishes. "I wish I could do this. I wish I could do that."

To succeed, we need to muster up immense willpower and extraordinary self-discipline. It is painful. It is hard. It is difficult. If you don't have a burning desire to succeed, if you aren't willing to die trying, you will not succeed.

The truth is that you can learn all of the willpower and self-discipline hacks you want. But until you find that one thing that ignites within you a raging, burning desire, you will never reach your full potential.

As Eric Thomas said:

*"When you want to succeed as bad as you want to breathe, then you'll be successful."*

When you have a desire that transcends all else, a life mission, a higher purpose, you will do whatever it takes. You will muster willpower you didn't realize you had and find self-discipline where previously there had been none.

## Commitment

You can't simply go through life telling yourself, "Wouldn't it be wonderful if I could do that one day... Wouldn't it be nice if I did that thing..."

You need to find something that you truly want, and then commit your very being to it. You must make a commitment to your goals.

Otherwise, you'll see no harm in slapping the snooze button for "just another 5 minutes..." when it goes off at 5am. Otherwise, you'll give up and quit that project when the initial rush of enthusiasm fades and the first sign of struggle appears.

The main reason that so many of us lack self-discipline and willpower is that we lack a compelling reason. It's not that we are inherently lazy or naturally unable to cope with difficulty. When we have a burning desire — a compelling reason for completing our goals, no matter how hard it gets — we can surmount anything. Just like the Navy SEALs with a higher purpose that came to the realization that they are capable of 20X what they had ever thought possible.

Most people don't commit to their goals. Most people don't have a compelling reason for sticking it out through the inevitable hardships required for success.

I've already mentioned this quote, but here it is just one more time. The power and wisdom of this quote cannot be overstated:

*"He who has a **'why'** to live for can bear almost any **'how'**."*
*— Friedrich Nietzsche*

# Chapter 3: Awareness

In the previous chapter, we discussed the importance of having a mission. A higher purpose. A *'why'*. Another reason that the importance of such a goal cannot be overstated is that it makes you more aware of your actions.

When you know where you want to be and have a burning desire to reach that goal, it floods your mind. You will begin judging your actions against your goal, without thinking. You will being to think, does doing this help me get to where I want to be? Does this help me? Will this move me forward?

Self-discipline is dependent upon you being aware of what you are and aren't doing. Without conscious awareness of your behavior — if you don't realize that you are being undisciplined — you won't know to act otherwise.

You'll just shrug your shoulders and tell yourself, "Nothing wrong with watching five hours of television each day. Everybody does it!"

However, if you a burning desire to start an online fashion brand or write a bestselling novel, you will look at yourself sitting on the couch and think, "Geez, this ain't exactly helping me reach my goals. Get off your ass you lazy wimp. Go do something productive. Work toward your goal."

As you start building self-discipline, you will catch yourself when you're acting undisciplined. Avoiding gym, eating cake, mindlessly browsing the web or compulsively checking emails.

It is this awareness of your own behavior that is necessary to begin working toward self-discipline. Furthermore, as will discuss Chapter Six, this awareness enables you to structure your life in a way that propels you toward your goals. Such things as removing potential traps by, for example, not having any junk food in the house.

The first step to building willpower and living with discipline is to realize when you are caving to temptation and a lust for instant-gratification. Discipline means that you behave in a way that reflects what you have decided is best, regardless of how you may feel in the heat of the moment.

Discipline means acting according to how you *think*, not how you *feel*. For this reason, the first step to building self-discipline is being aware of your behaviors, and whether or not they reflect your goals and ambitions.

This is why so many self-help gurus advocate writing down your goals or mission statement on a piece of paper or card and then reading it aloud to yourself upon arising in the morning and upon resting of a night. This keeps your goal at the forefront of your mind so that you are aware of when you are on track and when you are off track.

Once you know exactly what it is that you desire in life, everything else becomes so much easier.

The rest of this book is dedicated to making sure that you stay on track. Making sure that when you veer off course or feel that you don't have the will to continue, that you are able to power through with all your might regardless, and ultimately triumph.

# Chapter 4: State Management

*"There is always an inner game being played in your mind no matter what outer game you are playing. How you play this game usually makes the difference between success and failure."*
— *Tim Gallwey*

By far the most common reason that people don't get things done is that they "don't feel like it." The time isn't "just right." They'll do it when they feel motivated. When they feel good.

Remember that dog-tied-to-a-cart analogy?

Most people on this planet are like the dog being pulled around by the cart. If something bad happens, they feel bad, If something good happens, they feel good. If not much is happening, they just feel rather ordinary and "meh." They get dragged along wherever the cart goes. Their emotions — their inner state — is dependent on external events.

That is a terrible way to be. You have no control over external events, so why tie your emotions and motivation to the outside world? Do this and you will never get anything done. Most of the time, you will feel pretty ordinary and definitely won't feel ready to conquer the world and achieve your goals.

Instead, you need to master your internal state. You need to develop yourself and have your internal state — your emotions, feelings, and level of motivation — independent of external events. This is the key to self-discipline and willpower.

Why is it that we wish we could have more willpower? Why do we desire the ability to discipline ourselves?

I'll tell you why: So we can get stuff done.

We want more willpower so that can power through a lack of motivation and abundance of difficulty and get things done. We want more willpower so that we can get things done even when we don't feel motivated. We want willpower so that we do the things that we truly want to do, rather than succumb to instant gratification and unproductivity, feeling pangs of regret, guilt, and disappointment later on.

Well, there is one easy hack: Feel great on demand. Feel motivated whenever you choose to. Feel awesome each and every day.

Or, as a *Nike* advertisement once put it:

*"I'm coming back with a state of mind three coffees, two flirtatious emails and a week of vacation can't buy."*

So how can you feel like this on demand? How can we saturate our life with feelings of motivation, confidence, drive, and willpower?

By controlling our internal state. This is done by controlling our focus and physiology.

Let's delve into exactly how we can change our state of mind on demand.

<u>Physiology</u>

Every feeling, every emotion, every state of mind all have a specific physiology associated with it. The way we use our body.

For example, if you've just won a gold medal in the Olympics, you might shout triumphantly, beat your chest, tell yourself how great you are, pump your hands in the sky in victory, and do a victory lap. You feel great.

But that's not the end of the story.

If you get up off the couch after watching five hours of television, and go the exact same thing — shouting triumphantly, beating your chest to show the world how great you are, pump your hands up in victory, and run a victory lap around your house — you will end up feeling amazing.

As they say, *act as if.* Act as if you feel great, and you will feel great. Act as if you feel motivated and super pumped, and you will feel motivated and super pumped.

Sound too good to be true? Sound ridiculous?

Science proves it.

Harvard researchers — and countless other researchers and universities across the globe — have all proved it.

Most people assume that how we feel determines our body language and physiology. In other words, if you feel amazing, you will have confident, strong, happy body language. Likewise, if you feel terrible, your body language will reflect it.

While this is true, the researchers from Harvard Business School have shown that you can hijack this process. That the opposite is true, too. In other words, by pretending that you feel amazing, and having your body language reflect confidence, drive, and motivation, you will actually *feel* that way.

Furthermore, you don't just end up *feeling* better. You actually end up better! Your body releases hormones and chemicals in the brain that make you happy, confident and motivated — testosterone. They also found that levels of the hormone that produces stress and anxiety — cortisol — drop.

The researchers showed this by doing a study and having participants do either high-power poses or low-power poses.

High-power poses are such things as standing tall, taking up heaps of space, spreading out, relaxing, putting your feet up on the table, your hands behind your head, or your arm over another chair, and so on. Making yourself bigger. Taking up more space. Acting like a powerful, confident person.

Low-power poses included crossing your arms, crossing your legs, putting your hand on your neck or the side of your face, and just generally taking up less space and making yourself smaller. Acting like a weak, anxious person.

The results were that those who did the confident high-power poses saw their testosterone levels soar and their cortisol levels plummet. By acting confident and powerful, they actually became confident and powerful.

Conversely, those that did the weak, anxious low-power poses saw just the opposite. Their testosterone levels plummeted and their cortisol levels soared. By acting weak and anxious, they actually become weak and anxious.

Furthermore, and additional study was done which found that by doing high-power poses for two minutes before a job interview (even if it meant doing the high power poses in a bathroom stall so that they don't look like an idiot), employers were significantly more likely to chose them. Those that did low power poses (more common than you'd realize — slouching over your smartphone going over notes, anyone?) had a comparatively small chance.

What this means is that other people — the job interviewers in this case — can sense the feelings of confidence, drive, and motivation that resulted from doing the high-power poses beforehand.

Act like you are confident, and you will be confident. Start moving, standing, talking, breathing, and gesturing like powerful and successful people. By changing your physiology, you change your internal feelings and state of mind. Your body will lead your mind.

Tony Robbins is a huge advocate of state management, which he does by changing his physiology. As he said:

*"I don't hope I'm going to be in a good state, I demand it. So I do an incantation using my whole body."*

He advocates telling yourself super positive things, telling yourself how great you are, how awesome everything is going to be, and acting like it. Jump up and down, shout triumphantly. Act like it. As he said:

*"Speak it and embody what you are saying with all the intensity you can."*

Similarly, Jordan Belfort, more famously known as the real life Wolf of Wall Street, also swears by state management:

*"Some people think that the world happens to them. Bad things happen so I feel bad. Good things happen I feel good. No! That's flawed software.*

*"The way our brain works, you can feel any way you want to feel."*

Let's move on to the next aspect of state management: Focus — what you think about.

<u>Focus</u>

So many people in this world focus on negative things. It's incredible!

Whinging. Complaining. Worrying about things that are out of their control. This is so prevalent in fact, that in Stephen Covey's *The 7 Habits of Highly Effective People*, his first success habit was being proactive. What this means is rather than focusing on things beyond your control, such as "we have such stupid politicians! These dumb policies are hurting my business!" focus instead on the things that you can control.

No matter how good you are at complaining, it's not going to change anything. Instead, focus on what you can control. How can you make your product better? How can you best serve your customers needs?

The importance of what you focus on and think about goes beyond just being a highly effective person. What you focus on and think about also has a huge impact on your motivation, willpower, and self-discipline.

Do you want the willpower and motivation to do that thing you've been meaning to do for ages? Don't focus on what you can't control. Don't focus on negative things. Don't focus on why you cannot do it. Don't focus on excuses.

Instead, focus on positive things. Focus on why you can do it, focus on how you are going to do it, focus on what amazing job you're going to do of this task and how awesome it's going to be once you've succeeded in completing it. Focus on positive thoughts.

You know that negative little voice that's always in the back of your head complaining and telling you that you can't do it? Seize control of that voice. Start telling yourself positive things. Flood your mind with positive self-talk. Think about the great things in life.

Some people take this even further and download heaps of motivational audio programs to help keep their willpower and level of motivation sky high in perpetuity. Audiobooks and audio programs by such people as Earl Nightingale, Brian Tracy, Grant Cardone, Denis Waitley, and Zig Ziglar.

Download a bunch of these to your phone and listen to them for half an hour or so each day while you're doing some mindless activities — such as exercising, doing the washing, cooking, cleaning, and so on. It's not just the great ideas and information that these programs will fill you with, but it's the positive vibe, the contagious motivation and positive, empowering emotions and feelings. It's the attitude behind it all.

Do this, and you will find yourself increasingly focused, optimistic, and motivated. Your self-discipline and willpower will shoot through the roof as a result. You will be getting things done that you've previously delayed for eternity. You'll be able to resist temptation and pursue delayed gratification rather than succumbing to the allure of instant gratification.

Beat that voice in your head and you will be able to do anything.

As John C. Maxwell said:

*"You don't overcome challenges by making them smaller but by making yourself bigger."*

## All in All

Control what you focus on. Fill yourself up with positive self-talk. Flood your mind with positive vibes, successful attitudes, and motivating energy.

Control your physiology. Make your body language empowering. Act as if. Act like — and mimic the behaviors of — the triumphant, the powerful, and the successful.

Control your focus and physiology, and you will control your state of mind. You will control how you feel. You can go from feeling terrible, lazy, unmotivated, and lacking willpower, to feeling great, amazing, motivated, and full of willpower in under two minutes. All you need to do is control your thoughts and body. With that, you can manage your state. And when you can manage your state of mind, self-discipline becomes a breeze.

Feeling lazy, unmotivated, undisciplined, and lacking willpower? I know that feeling personally. It is almost always after a big day of work. I go sit on the couch and mindlessly browse the web, watch a television show and indulge in not the healthiest of foods. I feel like I've had a huge day and exhausted and depleted of all energy and willpower.

When I feel like this, I get up, turn on some loud rock music (AC/DC is my favorite), grab a glass of ice cold water, and groove with the beat of the rock music. I do some push ups, pulls ups, and get moving, beat my chest like King Kong, and tell myself how great I am. Before I know it — just a few minutes later — I feel ready to smash through another pile of work. I feel reinvigorated and refreshed as though I just woke up from an awesome night's rest.

The reality is that I didn't just wake up from a great night's rest. But my brain doesn't know the difference. I start acting like I'm pumped and motivated, and within a minute or two, my brain starts releasing heaps of positive chemicals and hormones to reflect how I'm acting.

By pretending to be pumped and motivated, I actually become super pumped and motivated. Even though just a few moments earlier I felt like shit, felt completely exhausted and absent of any sort of motivation, energy, or willpower

The power of state management cannot be overstated. In fact, a 2012 study titled _Masters of the Long Haul_ found that state management is the single most important factor for success and for achieving your long-term goals. By mastering state management, you enable yourself to overcome difficulties and setbacks and keep on going. You enable yourself to keep on working hard, even if you're not "in the mood" or don't feel up to it.

# Chapter 5: Health and Lifestyle

A necessity for strong willpower, and consequently self-discipline, is health. That means having a healthy diet, getting enough sleep, and exercising regularly.

When you are in an unhealthy state, your willpower dissipates. A lack of sleep, an unhealthy body, or poor quality and unhealthy foods won't cut it. If you want to perform at your peak, you need to *be* at your peak.

Just like Olympians and star athletes make sure that they get enough sleep and eat all the right foods, you'll find that the world's wealthiest and most powerful people — such as CEOs and world leaders — do just the same. Healthy diet, enough sleep, and regular exercise. They treat performing at their mental peak like athletes treat performing at their physical peak.

In fact, studies have shown that a low blood sugar level weakens your resolve. If you're hungry or stuffed full of junk food, your ability to concentrate and focus suffers as your brain is not functioning at its peak. Furthermore, you'll probably be grumpy and pessimistic, too. Your self-discipline slips away and your willpower evaporates.

To have your brain function at its highest potential, you need to be at your physical peak. As President John F. Kennedy said:

*"Physical fitness is not only one of the most important keys to a healthy body, it is the basis of dynamic and creative intellectual activity."*

When you are tired, hungry, and physically unfit, your motivation, self-discipline, and willpower all go out the window.

Furthermore, regular exercise strengthens your willpower by getting the blood flowing through your body and brain. The additional oxygen and nutrients that make their way to the brain boost its function. Exercise also naturally stimulates the release of hormones in the body which give you confidence, make you feel great, and boost your willpower.

Regarding exercise, many great inventors and geniuses have been known for regularly going on long walks. From Beethoven to Steve Jobs, from Nikola Tesla to Charles Dickens, from Mark Zuckerberg to Charles Darwin. Going on walks has been scientifically proven to boost creativity and productivity, and moreover, you come back to what you're working on with a fresh set of eyes. You are refreshed, and your willpower replenished.

As willpower can be depleted, the successful among us make a habit of healthy eating and daily exercise. This way, they are not depleting their willpower — it's just a habit.

The best way to maintain high levels of willpower is to make habits. This way, your willpower is saved for the tasks that need it the most.

This talk of habits and automating tasks to conserve willpower brings us to the next chapter.

# Chapter 6: Structuring Life

Willpower is exhausted through use. It is depleted over the course of the day. What this means is that if you do lots of little things that exhaust your willpower, you'll quickly run out before the day is over, and thus not perform at your peak.

There is, however, one way that we can conserve willpower.

How's that?

We can conserve our willpower by structuring our life in a way that reduces the need to expend our willpower. You can do this by creating habits and removing temptations.

## Creating Habits

What do the world's most powerful man, the youngest person to ever become a billionaire, the founder of the world's most valuable and profitable company, the world's most successful director, and *Time* magazine's "Person of the Century" all have in common?

That would be President Barack Obama (President of the United States), Mark Zuckerberg (Facebook founder and CEO), Steve Jobs (Apple founder), Christopher Nolan (director of the Dark Knight trilogy, Interstellar, and Inception), and Albert Einstein (most influential physicist in history).

So what do all these highly successful chaps have in common?

They all wear the same outfit each day.

President Obama said the following regarding the lack of diversity in his wardrobe:

*"You'll see I wear only gray or blue suits. I'm trying to pare down decisions."*

Likewise, Mark Zuckerberg said the following of his unwavering commitment to grey t-shirts and blue jeans:

*"I really want to clear my life to make it so that I have to make as few decisions as possible about anything except how to best serve this community [Facebook]."*

Similarly, Christopher Nolan had the following to say:

*"It's just what I'm comfortable in. I don't like to think about what to wear, so I just wear the same thing every day."*

These are some of the world's most successful individuals. They are so determined to make the most of their willpower that they streamline their lives to that extent. They don't even worry themselves about choosing what to wear each day.

Studies show that there is an interrelationship between willpower depletion and decision fatigue. Decision fatigue refers to the deteriorating quality of decisions made by a person after making lots of previous decisions. Therefore, your ability for self-control against impulses decreases in the face of decision fatigue. By making lots of decisions — such as stressing over what to wear — you deplete your willpower.

Even grocery stores are aware of this. Grocery stores are often designed to profit off our depleted willpower. Nathan DeWall, professor of psychology and self-regulation expert at the University of Kentucky said the following of grocery stores:

*"They don't put produce by the checkout for a reason. They know you've just made a bunch of decisions; they know you're exhausted, so that's where they put the junk food."*

While you can't change the layout of your supermarket (although you could do an online order), you do have control over the environment at home and at work. For example, if you have no sweets or junk food at home, you don't need exhaust willpower by choosing to eat healthy. If you only have healthy food at home, sticking to your diet literally requires zero willpower. That willpower is then saved for the more important tasks that you will tackle throughout the rest of the day.

As they say, "out of sight, out of mind."

This same method can be applied to countless other temptations that you might otherwise find yourself succumbing to. If you find yourself wasting time on Facebook when you should be working, you can turn off the internet while working or download a browser extension that blocks certain websites for set amount of time. If you find yourself eating unhealthy food at work for lunch, get the intern to remove you from the lunch email. If you find yourself overspending while shopping, leave your cards at home and just take a set amount of cash.

## Path of Least Resistence

A stunning example of this method has to do with organ donation. Rather than just eliminating cookies from your diet by having none in the house, it has been shown that countries were the majority of people as organ donors are the countries where that is the default option. The countries where you need to tick the form to become an organ donor have extraordinarily few organ donors. The countries where you need to tick the form to *exclude* yourself form the organ donor program have almost the entire population as organ donors.

Simply having organ donation as either the default or non-default choice on the form had that big of an impact!

The lesson we can learn from this is that convenience is key. We humans have evolved to conserve energy. We almost always take the path of least resistance.

Cookies in the house? We'll eat them. No cookies? Well, it's not like we're going to drive all the way to the shops just to go buy a packet. Is the majority of your country organ donors?

Depends whether or not they had to tick the box.

Author of *The Happiness Advantage* Shawn Archer decided to take advantage of the fact that we humans tend to take the path of least resistance. Archer had always been meaning to learn guitar, but he struggled to maintain the discipline required to practice each and every day. Most evenings he just turned on the television instead.

So what did he do?

Realizing that it was far easier to just watch TV than it was to start practicing guitar, he put his guitar in an easy to reach spot and removed the batteries from the TV remote. By doing this, he successfully got himself to start practicing guitar.

## Morning Magic

Many of the globe's most powerful and successful people make a habit of exercising each morning.

Morning? Why the morning? Why not after work?

Well, these ultra successful individuals realize the importance of daily exercise. They know that it is essential to their well being, productivity, and performance. They also know that after a big tiring day at work, after having depleted all their willpower, they probably won't feel like going to the gym.

So, aware of the extraordinary importance of exercise, they do it of a morning, before their willpower is depleted and before there are any distractions vying for their attention.

You can apply this to your own life, too. Not necessarily just for exercise, either. If you've got a business that you'd love to start, or a novel that you've always been wanting to write, then wake up an hour or two earlier, and do it then!

Schedule It

Studies show that if you schedule a task that you want to do, you will almost certainly do it. In the study, researchers told one group of all of the benefits of exercise, and the harms of inactivity. The researchers then told them to make sure that they exercised.

The researchers told the other group to schedule a specific time and place that they would exercise, as well as what sort of exercise they would do. They were to write it down.

Of the group told lectured on the benefits of exercise and harms of inactivity, very few participants actually exercised. Of the group that scheduled their exercise, the majority followed through and actually exercised.

The key lesson is this: If you want to do something, schedule it! Have a plan.

Presumably, by scheduling and planning their exercise, they eliminated the need to make a decision or devote willpower to get them to start exercising. They had already made their decision. That was what they were going to do. So they just went down the path of least resistance, did what they planned, and thus exercised.

Other research, unrelated to exercise, has revealed that when your willpower gets depleted, having a plan and a goal that you are pursuing mitigates the impact of decreased willpower.

## One at a Time

As we have discussed in depth earlier on in this book, willpower is finite. It can be depleted. This means that we must incorporate an important idea into how we structure our life.

Only work on one goal at a time. If you work on more, you will spread your willpower too thinly. By working on one thing, you less willpower available for other things. Therefore, if you attempt to work on multiple goals or habits simultaneously, you commit yourself to almost certain failure.

Focus on one goal or habit at a time and you shall succeed. Funnel all of your willpower fuel toward one thing.

# Conclusion

*"Promise me you'll always remember: You're braver than you believe, and stronger than you seem, and smarter than you think."*
— *Christopher Robin to Winnie the Pooh*

Self-discipline is essential to conquering your goals and achieving your ambitions. Here is a brief summary on how you can develop *Iron Willpower*:

**1. Willpower as a Muscle:** Don't see willpower as something you either have or do not have. Rather, view it as a muscle. Just as a bodybuilder knows that even if he can't lift a certain weight today, he will eventually be able to lift it if he consistently develops his muscles.

Go about your life not in despair of your seemingly weak willpower, but in search of ways to strengthen your willpower, increase your self-discipline, and build grit and strength of character. Know within your heart that as you continuously develop yourself and exert willpower you will become better and better. You will build iron-like willpower.

**2. Be on a Mission:** Be on a mission. Have a big life goal. When you have a burning desire to achieve an immense — yet specific — goal, you will find yourself capable of doing what is necessary to achieve that ideal you hold deep within your heart.

**3. Awareness:** Having an overarching goal will also make you more aware of what you should and shouldn't be doing, and thus, help put you on the right track and increase your self-discipline.

**4. State Management:** When you feel lazy and unmotivated, realize that you can change your state of mind by changing your physiology and focus.

**5. Health and Lifestyle:** Eat healthy and exercise regularly. Not only will this make you feel better, but you will also perform better and be much, much, much more productive. Moreover, studies show that building discipline in one area of life — such as regular exercise and healthy eating — leads to significantly increased self-discipline in other areas of life as well.

**6. Structuring Life:** Finally, make the most of habits. Create habits that propel you toward success so that you are productive and self-disciplined on autopilot, without even thinking. Structure your life for self-discipline and success.

To conclude, here are a few quotes relating to self-discipline from two of history's wisest men.

*"It had long since come to my attention that people of accomplishment rarely sat back and let things happen to them. They went out and happened to things."*
*— Leonardo da Vinci*

*"You have power over your mind — not outside events. Realize this, and you will find strength."*

*— Marcus Aurelius, Roman Emperor*

*"One can have no smaller or greater mastery than mastery of oneself."*
*— Leonardo da Vinci,*

Made in the USA
Columbia, SC
03 September 2017